Then there were none

Then there were none

Martha H. Noyes

Based on the documentary film by
Elizabeth Kapuʻuwailani Lindsey Buyers, Ph.D.

BessPress.com

Design: Carol Colbath

Noyes, Martha H.
   Then there were none / Martha
H. Noyes ; based on the
documentary film by Elizabeth
Kapuʻuwailani Lindsey Buyers.
       p. cm.
   Includes illustrations,
bibliography.
   ISBN 978-1-57306-155-1
   1. Hawaii - History.
2. Indigenous peoples - Hawaii.
3. Hawaiians - Ethnic identity.
I. Buyers, Elizabeth Kapuʻuwailani
Lindsey. II. Title.
DU625.N69 2003   996.9-dc21

Printed in China

The excerpts on pages 5 and 15 are reprinted by permission of the
University of Chicago Press from *The Kumulipo: A Hawaiian
Creation Chant,* translated and edited with commentary by Martha
Warren Beckwith, Honolulu: University of Hawaiʻi Press, 1972,
© 1951 by The University of Chicago.

Reprinted 2021

To the five thousand *piha kānaka maoli*
who remain

Foreword

Then There Were None was born from unspoken words, unshed tears, and wounded spirits. It is not a tale of blame or victimization. It is an effort to give voice to *kūpuna* who became strangers in their own land, a land that once nourished their dreams and now cradles their bones. Without these stories, Hawai'i's history is incomplete.

My *kuleana*, my life's work, is humbly devoted to remembering our *kūpuna*, upon whose shoulders I stand. Through my work and the work of people such as my colleague and friend Martha Noyes and my husband, J. W. A. Buyers, who produced the documentary film *Then There Were None*, silence will not shroud our future generations. They will know who they are, from whence they come, and the sounds of all the world's voices.

Me ka ha'aha'a a me ke aloha,
Elizabeth Kapu'uwailani Lindsey Buyers, Ph.D.

$\mathscr{P}$reface

Then There Were None is not a history text. In neither the film nor the book have we attempted objectivity.

What drove our work was the absence of material expressing the *experience* of being Hawaiian during the last two hundred years. And why should that matter? Because it is the legacy of emotions and feelings that shape Hawaiian issues today.

History, like statistics, can be bent, argued, and interpreted to fit any point of view. But the language of the heart, the sounds of the spirit, are beyond argument. They were what they were, they are what they are.

Look at any newspaper. Irish Catholics and Irish Protestants, Chechnyans and Russians, Tutsis and Hutus, Indian Hindus and Indian Moslems, Israelis and Palestinians. Has any history text, however objective, quelled the troubles between them?

No, because history isn't what divides them. What fuels the division is emotion.

It is an emotional voice we wanted to offer. If the heart's wounds, the spirit's ache are laid bare, healing balm can reach the injury and ease the pain.

There is no blame, no guilt. There is only the responsibility each of us chooses to recognize the pain and heal the wound.

We are all in this together. We share the legacy and we share the present. And we share the shaping of our children's future.

$\mathcal{W}$e have been in these islands for two thousand years. For thousands of years before that we have been Pacific Island people.

Archaeologists and anthropologists argue over what date the first people came to these Hawaiian islands. Remains have been found that date to 150 BC. We have been here a long time.

*T*he world knows of our green mountains and blue seas. The world knows of swaying hula dancers and of Pearl Harbor. The world knows of pineapples, mai tais, Kona coffee, and macadamia nuts. The world knows of coco palms and white sand beaches, of flower leis and brightly colored mu'umu'us.

But the world does not know of us. We are Hawaiian. This is our story.

In the Beginning

O ke au i kahuli wela ka honua

At the time when the earth became hot

O ke au i kahuli lole ka lani

At the time when the heavens turned about

O ke au i kuka'iaka ka la

At the time when the sun was darkened

E ho'omalamalama i ka malama

To cause the moon to shine

O ke au i Makali'i ka po

The time of the rise of the Pleiades

O ka Walewale ho'okumu honua ia

The slime, this was the source of the earth

O ke kumu o ka lipo

The source of the darkness that made darkness

O ke kumu a ka Po i po ai

The source of the night that made night

O ka lipolipo, o ka lipolipo

The intense darkness, the deep darkness

O ka lipo o ka La, o ka lipo o ka Po

Darkness of the sun, darkness of the night

Po wale ho-i

Nothing but night

—Prologue to the *Kumulipo*, the Hawaiian chant of creation

*O*urs is a culture rooted in a cosmology both simple and profound. The heart, the seat, the center of our cosmology is the interwoven three-part unity of nature, man, and deity. For any one of the three to be healthy and prosper, each must be in its proper relationship with the rest. The life of each depends on the life of all.

> *Ua mau ka ea o ka ʻāina i ka pono.*
> The life of the land is perpetuated
> in righteousness.

*I*n January 1778 British Captains James Cook and George Vancouver sailed their ships *Discovery* and *Resolution* into Kealakekua Bay on the island of Hawai'i. Because it was the season of the annual Makahiki Festival, dedicated to the god Lono as Lono-i-ka-Makahiki, who long ago sailed away with a promise to return; because the sails of the English ships resembled the white *kapa* banners of Lono; because the English vessels were so big as to be like the floating islands on which Lono-i-ka-Makahiki said he would come back; and because Kealakekua, the place where the English arrived, means The-Pathway-of-the-God. Cook was greeted with the ceremony and respect due a returning sacred chief.

But when the season of the Makahiki ended, the English were still there. They were mortals, not gods. A disagreement arose between the chiefs of Hawai'i and the chiefs of England. Captain Cook was killed.

Vancouver sailed away with Cook's remains to return the bones of that chief to their native land. But behind them the British left an invisible and deadly enemy.

They left disease.

In 1778 there were between 400,000 and 1,000,000
Hawaiians in these islands.
By 1822 there were only 200,000 pure Hawaiians left alive.

*T*here was another legacy left by Cook, a legacy equally insidious as the bequest of disease. It was the germ of foreign influence, which rapidly and almost fatally turned into an epidemic of foreign domination.

In the first forty-two years after Cook, white whalers, traders, and adventurers plied their wares, spread their diseases, introduced whiskey, rum, and the Christian God, bartered for women and goods with cannons, muskets, swords, and the tools and trinkets of their own culture.

We welcomed the technology. Our culture has never been static; it has always been eager to acquire new knowledge, new understanding, and new ways to better manage our human responsibilities in the three-part unity upon which all life depends.

We were building a new and united Hawaiian nation. Kamehameha, a chief of Hawai'i island who had known Captains Cook and Vancouver in Kealakekua in 1778, had by 1810 united our islands under a single rule.

In 1819 Kamehameha died. He was succeeded by his son Liholiho, Kamehameha II, although in fact it was Ka'ahumanu, the most powerful of Kamehameha's wives, who ruled the kingdom as its first *kuhina nui*.

In 1820 the first American missionaries arrived.

O kane ia Waiʻololi, o ka wahine ia Waiʻolola
Man for the narrow stream, woman for the broad stream

. . . .

He po uheʻe i ka wawa
Darkness slips into light
He nuku, he wai ka ʻai a ka laʻau
Earth and water are the food of the plant
A ke Akua ke komo, ʻaoʻe komo kanaka
The god enters, man cannot enter.

—from the *Kumulipo*

$\mathcal{F}$ertility, fecundity, procreation. These were the wealth of our land.

But now we were dying. Babies were stillborn. Conception failed to occur. Healthy adults thrust themselves into the sea to drown their despair along with their lives.

Venereal disease, measles, influenza, the common cold—one epidemic after another, and our Hawaiian people had no immunity to these diseases, which had never before exposed themselves in Polynesian lands.

$\mathscr{B}$y 1828 there were only 188,000 pure Hawaiians left alive.

To the American Board of Missions
Boston, Massachusetts

*D*ear Brethren,

In this distant land of strangers, and of pagan darkness, it is a comfort to us to look back to that radiating
point of missionary light and love. . . . We rejoice, that
we have been allowed to walk over the ashes of idols,
and, in the name of our God, to set up our banners on
the ruins of pagan altars of abomination. But the nation,
as such, still lies in the ruins of the fall, with all its
native depravity, corrupted and debased by the dregs of
civilized society; and though many are disposed to look
favorably upon the message which we bring, and a few
seem to hail it with joy, it is by no means improbable,
that when it shall be generally perceived that the gospel
will require them to give up all their sinful lusts, that a
great struggle will be made to resist or to shake off such
claims.

—signed February 20, 1821, by Hiram Bingham and Asa Thurston, of
the first party of American missionaries

We had no concept of original sin. To our way of thinking the natural functions of life and life's pleasures and enjoyments were respect and homage to deity. Pain and suffering came about when the three-part unity of nature, man, and gods was out of order. We sought in our prayers and offerings to maintain the harmony of life.

Our traditions have many ways to express the reverence and respect for our deities. Nearly every one of our most deeply rooted traditions was looked upon as evil by these newly arrived Christian missionaries.

Many of our people welcomed the Christian gods. This was not so extraordinary a thing for us. To welcome a new deity was an age-old practice. And it was clear that the Christian god, and his family of Jesus and Mary and the Holy Ghost and the saints, was a god of some *mana,* some great power.

We have always known that words contain *mana.* Our Hawaiian language recognizes the power of words in their literal sense, their metaphoric sense, and their symbolic sense.

With the missionary God came words as physical form, embodied in ink on pages of writing. This was something of great value.

$\mathcal{M}$ANA

Supernatural or divine power, mana, miraculous power;
a powerful nation, authority; to give mana to, to make
powerful; to have mana, power, authority; authoriza-
tion, privilege; miraculous, divinely powerful; possessed
of man, power.

$\mathcal{H}$O'OMANA

To place in authority, empower, authorize. To worship.

—from Mary Kawena Pukui and Samuel H. Elbert,
Hawaiian Dictionary

*W*e wanted reading and writing, but we wanted to add them to what we had, not to replace our own traditions, but rather to strengthen our understanding, increase our knowledge, and express our part in the three-fold unity of nature, man, and gods.

This three-fold unity is the macrocosmic triune essence. In microcosm it is reflected in the human being. In the individual it is body, mind, and spirit. And the two, the macrocosmic and the microcosmic, are interlinked, both vertically and horizontally. The body corresponds to nature, the mind to man, the spirit to deity. And for the person to play a proper part in the whole, body, mind, and spirit must be in internal balance and in harmony with nature and deity.

Our traditions derive from the balancing of these unities. We disciplined ourselves to express in our arts and practices the respect and recognition of the unity as sacred, and to acknowledge our place and part within it.

Hula is one of the most important of these expressions.

*H*U-LA

hū: To rise or swell, overflow, percolate, effervesce, boil over; to surge or rise to the surface, as emotion; swelling, outburst, to overflow.

lā: Sun, heat, sunny. Day. Symbolically light, which in turn is symbolically knowledge, enlightenment, life.

lā: There, then, that.

la'a: Sacred, holy, devoted, consecrated, set aside for sacred purposes, dedicated.

—from Mary Kawena Pukui and Samuel H. Elbert,
Hawaiian Dictionary; and the teachings of
Pilahi Paki

The hula was a religious service, in which poetry, music, pantomime, and the dance lent themselves, under the forms of dramatic art, to the refreshment of men's minds. Its view of life was idyllic, and it gave itself to the celebration of those mythical times when gods and goddesses moved on earth as men and women and when men and women were as gods.

—Nathaniel B. Emerson, *Unwritten Literature of Hawai'i:*
The Sacred Songs of the Hula

We learned that Mr. Charles H. Derby went over to San Francisco by the *Comet,* taking with him some native men and women, for the purpose of opening an exhibition in that city. A man must be pretty hard up for employment to undertake an exhibition of these islanders and their disgusting dances in a civilized country and to a refined community.

—*Pacific Commercial Advertiser,* March 1862

Laka, the obscene goddess, still presides over the unspeakable abominations of the hula.

—J.S. Emerson, "The Lesser Hawaiian Gods," *Hawaiian Historical Society Papers,* April 7, 1892

$\mathcal{B}$y 1836 there were 108,000 pure
Hawaiians left alive.

$\mathcal{T}$he assault of Western culture upon Hawaiian culture drove deeper and harder as the 1800s marched on. By 1839 the government of our kingdom, though still headed by kings and *kuhina nui* of the Kamehameha dynasty, was in fact controlled by American missionaries and their merchant friends who had had themselves appointed to cabinet and advisory posts.

In 1840 Kauikeaouli, Kamehameha III, established the first constitution of the kingdom. In 1848 the Western ax blade cut sharply into the neck of the Hawaiian cultural body.

Kamehameha III, at the insistence and with the politically engineered manipulations of foreign advisors—Dr. Gerrit P. Judd, an American missionary; Robert C. Wyllie, a Scotland-born merchant; William L. Lee, an American lawyer; Richard Armstrong, an American missionary; Charles G. Hopkins, an English businessman; and Lorrin Andrews, an American missionary—promulgated the Mahele, dividing the lands of our islands into three parts. One part was reserved for the king and his heirs, one part was for the government, and one part was to be distributed among the Hawaiian people.

Two years later, in 1850, the Mahele was amended at the urging of these same advisors to allow foreigners to purchase Hawaiian land in fee simple. The lifeblood of Hawai'i flowed out like water from a broken gourd.

"*Their* customs and manner of treating one another show a primitive generosity which is truly delightful and which is often a reproach to our own people. Whatever one has, they all have. Money, food, clothes, they share with one another, even to the last piece of tobacco to put in their pipes. I once heard old 'Mr. Bingham' [a Hawaiian man] say with the highest indignation to a Yankee trader who was trying to persuade him to keep his money to himself: 'No! We no all 'e same a you! Suppose one got money, all got money; you—suppose one got money, lock him up in chest; no good. Kanaka all 'e same one.' This principle they carry so far that none of them will eat anything in sight of the others without offering it all around. I have seen one of them break a biscuit which had been given him, in five parts, at a time when I knew he was on a very short allowance, as there was but little to eat on the beach."

—Richard Henry Dana, c. 1859, quoted in
Ed Towse, "Some Hawaiians Abroad," *Papers of
the Hawaiian Historical Society* (11, 1904)

$\mathcal{P}$apa is the goddess of the earth, and her name means "foundation." She is Papa-hānau-moku, Papa-from-whom-lands-are-born. Wākea is her mate.

Wakea son of Kahiko-lua-mea,
Papa, called Papa-giving-birth-to-islands, was his wife,
Eastern Kahiki, western Kahiki were born,
The regions below were born,
The regions above were born,
Hawai'i was born,
The firstborn child was the island of Hawai'i,
Of Wakea together with Kane,
And Papa in the person of Walinu'u as wife.
Papa became pregnant with the island,
Sick with the foetus she bore,
Great Maui was born, an island
Papa was in heavy travail with the island Kanaloa,
A child born to Papa.
Papa left and returned to Tahiti,
Went back to Tahiti at Kapakapakaua,
Wakea stayed, lived with Kaula as wife,
Lana'i kaula was born,
The firstborn of that wife.

Wakea sought a new wife and found Hina,
Hina lived as wife to Wakea,
Hina became pregnant with the island of Moloka'i,
The island of Moloka'i was a child of Hina.
The messenger of Kaula told
Of Wakea's living with another woman;
Papa was raging with jealousy,
Papa returned from Tahiti
Bitter against her husband Wakea,
Lived with Lua, a new husband,
O'ahu son of Lua was born,
O'ahu of Lua, an island child,
A child of Lua's youth.
She lived again with Wakea,
Conceived by him,
Became with the island of Kaua'i,
The island Kama-wae-lua-lani was born,
Ni'ihau was an afterbirth,
Lehua a boundary,
Kaula the last
Of the low reef islands of Lono.

—from *the Kumulipo*, in Abraham Fornander,
An Account of the Polynesian Race, vol. 1.

*P*ō is the world of dark formlessness of potentiality, the realm of the female principle. Lā is the sun; it is light, and light is the male principle that impregnates. Form is born, visible, alive, and active and lives out its time on earth in life until in death it returns to Pō, to formlessness, to spirit, and once again to potentiality.

In our cosmology, spirit gives birth to form.

*W*e had no notion of private property. The concept was, in fact, unthinkable. And as to land, well, how could it be that land could be alienated from the three-part unity of nature, man, and deity?

The word in Hawaiian for land is *'āina.*

'AI-NA

'ai: Food, plant food; to eat; to taste; edible.
-na: Passive/imperative suffix.

And we are *kama'āina,* children of the land.

But now we were cut off from the parent, severed from the land.

How could we grow food to feed ourselves? How could we gather wood to cook what food we had? How could we make thatch to house ourselves? How could we weave plant fiber nets to catch fish?

We were separated from the resources necessary for physical subsistence, and we were alienated from one-third of the heretofore inviolable unity upon which life itself depended.

Now both three-part unities were damaged. The person was not whole, not in harmony in his own unity of body, mind, and spirit. And the universe was not whole, was without harmony among nature, man, and god.

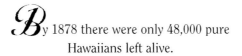

$\mathscr{B}$y 1878 there were only 48,000 pure
Hawaiians left alive.

$\mathcal{T}$he fall came quickly after that. Hawaiian land was claimed and purchased, not by Hawaiians but by Americans and Europeans.

Sugar was fast becoming king, and white plantation owners, whose livelihood was tied to trade with the United States, exerted ever-greater pressure on our government. In 1876 pressure on King David Kalākaua from white plantation owners and business interests resulted in the signing of the Reciprocity Treaty with the United States. This treaty gave Hawai'i "favored nation" status, ridding sugar exports from Hawai'i of duties and tariffs in trade with the United States, thus increasing sugar's profitability in the islands. In return for this boon, the Reciprocity Treaty required that Hawai'i allow no nation other than the United States the use of Pearl Harbor.

This concession of Pearl Harbor was a partial concession of Hawaiian sovereignty and at home it rankled. Sugar owners and other American interests in the islands were bolstered, but our native people were hurt and saddened. The foreign blade sank deeper into the Hawaiian heart.

In 1887 a white political group, the Hawaiian League, in command of several hundred armed white foot soldiers called the Honolulu Rifles, marched on 'Iolani Palace and forced Kalākaua's signature on a new constitution, quickly dubbed the Bayonet Constitution. The Bayonet Constitution curbed the rights and powers of the Monarch, reducing the king to more figurehead than ruler. This new constitution also required that the right to vote be vested only in those male residents who owned a minimum of three thousand dollars worth of property or who had a minimum annual income of at least six hundred dollars. Those requirements eliminated two-thirds of Hawai'i's population, and the overwhelming majority of the thus qualified one-third were white.

$\mathscr{B}$y 1890 there were only 39,000 pure Hawaiians left alive.

$\mathcal{K}$alākaua died in 1891. He was succeeded on the throne by his sister, Lydia Paki Liliʻuokalani. The queen chafed at the restraints of the Bayonet Constitution. She took as her motto *ʻOnipaʻa*—stand firm—and made it clear to all Hawaiʻi that she stood firm against any further Americanizing of the nation.

This prospect displeased the white plutocracy who had instigated and supported the Bayonet Constitution. In January of 1893 the queen announced her plan to promulgate a new constitution, one that would restore the power of the Hawaiian throne and the rights of the Hawaiian people.

In response, the all-white Annexationist Club, led by ardent pro-annexationist missionary descendant Lorrin A. Thurston, formed the Committee of Safety, the clear and overt purpose of which was to overthrow the Hawaiian monarchy and secure annexation of Hawaiʻi to the United States. To this end Thurston and the Committee of Safety gained the support of John L. Stevens, the United States minister in Hawaiʻi, and the armed U.S. Marines from the American gunship U.S.S. *Boston*.

On January 17, 1893, the Hawaiian monarchy was overthrown, replaced at first by an all-white Provisional Government and then in 1894 by an all-white government of the Republic of Hawaii. The Republic made application to Congress for U.S. territorial status, and in 1898 that status was conferred.

It was as though we had been consumed.

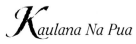

$\mathcal{K}$aulana Na Pua

(written by Helen Keho'ohiwaokalani Prendergast in 1893)

Kaulana na pua a'o Hawai'i
>   Famous are the children of Hawai'i
Kupa'a mahope o ka 'aina
>   Ever loyal to the land
Hiki mai ka 'elele o ka loko 'ino
>   When the evil-hearted messenger comes
Palapala 'anunu me ka pakaha
>   With his greedy document of extortion.

Pane mai Hawai'i moku o Keawe
>   Hawai'i, land of Keawe, answers
Kokua na Hono a'o Pi'ilani
>   Pi'ilani's bays help
Kako'o mai Kaua'i o Mano
>   Mano's Kaua'i lends support
Pa'apu me ke one Kakuhihewa
>   And so do the sands of Kakuhihewa.
'A'ole 'a'e kau i ka pulima
>   No one will fix a signature
Maluna o ka pepa o ka 'enemi
>   To the paper of the enemy

Hoʻohuhi ʻaina kuʻai hewa
    With its sin of annexation
I ka pono sivila aʻo ke kanaka
    And sale of native civil rights.

ʻAʻole makou aʻe minamina
    We do not value
I ka puʻu kala a ke aupuni
    The Government's sums of money
Ua lawa makou i ka pohaku
    We are satisfied with the stones
I ka ʻai kamahaʻo o ka ʻaina
    Astonishing food of the land.

Mahope makou o Liliʻulani
    We back Liliʻulani
A loaʻa ʻe ka pono o ka ʻaina
    Who has won the rights of the land
Haʻina ʻia mai ana ka puana
    Tell the story
Ka poʻe i aloha i ka ʻaina
    Of the people who love their land.

$\mathcal{A}$ paramount reason why annexation should not be long postponed is that, if it soon takes place, the crown and government lands will be cut up and sold to American and Christian people, thus preventing the Islands from being submerged and overrun by Asiatics.

—John L. Stevens, "A Plea for Annexation,"
The North American Review (157, December 1893)

$\mathcal{A}$t the "transfer of sovereignty" ceremony in 1898 and in the Organic Act of 1900 the control of Hawaiian land was placed in the hands of the government of the United States. Of the three land divisions created by the Mahele, much of the Crown Lands belonged to the Bishop Estate through Princess Bernice Pauahi Bishop, the last of the Kamehamehas; the lands for the common people were owned by whoever had purchased or gained title to them; and the government lands and the remainder of the Crown Lands became the Crown and Public Lands Trust, the trustee of which was the United States.

*N*ow, like it or not, we were American, and America made decisions, laws, and policies that were consistent with American aspirations. We were expected to assimilate, and if we did not, we were presumed disposable.

By property interests, commercial association, by school and political education, by the general prevalence of American laws, legal decisions, social and religious ideas, these Islands have become thoroughly Americanized. Go into the Chamber of Commerce, into the principal churches, into the courts, into the schools of Honolulu, Hilo and other chief towns in the Islands, and you would think yourself in New England or western New York. American ideas and interests are all dominant.

—John L. Stevens, "A Plea for Annexation,"
The North American Review (157, December 1983)

Speaking generally, a region larger than several of our States has been redeemed from utter savagery. . . . Tho [sic] the natives are steadily disappearing in number and seem likely sooner or later to disappear, their places are already supplied by others of sturdier stock.

—D.L. Leonard, D.D., "Christianity and the Hawaiian Islands," *The Missionary Review of the Word* (16, July 1903)

$\mathcal{A}$s a business asset, as a national playground and as the key to peace in the Pacific, Hawai'i is of tremendous importance.

—Lorrin A. Thurston, "Hawai'i—What It Means to America," *Sunset Magazine* (January 1926)

*O*ur very concept of ourselves was challenged. English was the language of education, and teachers punished our children if they spoke Hawaiian. Hawaiian scholar Mary Kawena Pukui (1895–1986) told a story of her experience as a boarding school student at

Honolulu's Mid-Pacific Institute. Kawena, half-Hawaiian and half-white, was fluent in both Hawaiian and English, but some of the new boarders at Mid-Pacific spoke only Hawaiian. One girl in particular had trouble understanding the teacher. Kawena turned to this student and translated the teacher's English-language instructions into Hawaiian. For this Kawena was physically punished and told not to speak her native tongue again.

Kawena's revenge was to become the greatest scholar of things Hawaiian this century has known. She wrote fifty-two books and articles, composed more than one hundred and fifty chants and meles (Hawaiian songs), was a translator, a genealogist, a storyteller, a chanter, and a linguist. With Samuel Elbert she coauthored the *Hawaiian Dictionary,* which, since the publication of its first edition in 1957, has been *the* dictionary of the Hawaiian language.

But the Americanizing dug deeper than official disapproval of our language. Many Hawaiian parents, concerned for their children's future, would not allow their own children to speak Hawaiian at all. And it wasn't just the Hawaiian language that was being suppressed. It was Hawaiian ways.

I must thank my father for saying that "You will be living in the *haole* time, and the wise thing to do is to move with the time, because time is a thing that belongs to no one. . . . There's only one thing I ask of you, my children—You are Hawai'i, and I would appreciate that you remain Hawai'i."

—Pilahi Paki (1910–1985)

*H*ollywood "discovered" Hawai'i in 1913 with the making of two movies, *Hawaiian Love* and *The Shark God*. A new and fantastic Hawai'i was born in American minds: exotic, romantic, at once idyllic and savage, mystical and superstitious, majestic and primitive, wise and silly, and always in the end succumbing to the mastery and virtue of the white hero or heroine of the story.

*I*n 1901 the Moana, the first of Hawai'i's grand hotels, opened its doors. In 1903 the Territory established a Board of Immigration to encourage mainland Americans to move to Hawai'i. In 1917 the Halekūlani Hotel opened. In 1919 the dredging of the Ala Wai Canal began, draining the wetlands of Waikīkī to make more land available for development, and the Hawaii Tourist Bureau campaigned to attract tourism to the Islands. In 1922 James D. Dole's Hawaiian Pineapple Company purchased the entire island of Lāna'i.

In 1927, on the site of what had once been a training ground for our high chiefs, the Royal Hawaiian Hotel opened with the pomp and ceremony due the new queen. The only Hawaiians present were the entertainers, the hotel help, and what remained of the royal family.

In the movies, on postcards and posters, in the magazines and travel journals, Hawai'i was romantic, languid, tranquil, gentle, and dramatic, but with all the conveniences and luxuries of America. Movie stars, businessmen, dignitaries, and the wealthy came to visit, to rest, and to explore in comfort our exotic American islands.

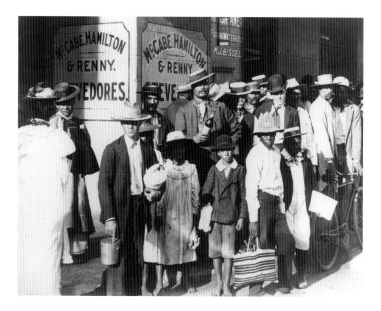

*B*ut our Hawaiian people were in trouble. Many, no longer able to continue their customary subsistence way of life, drifted to Honolulu, to find work on the docks or on the streets of the city. In the countryside, poverty ruled.

*H*awaiian delegate to Congress Prince Jonah Kūhiō Kalaniana'ole, a nephew of the queen, feared for the future of the Hawaiian people. At his urging, in 1920 Congress adopted the Hawaiian Homes Commission Act, which set aside 200,000 acres of land to be allocated to persons of 50 percent or more Hawaiian blood. The hope was that on these lands Hawaiian people could return to subsistence farming and to their cultural traditions and thus remain a viable and healthy people.

But the lands thus allocated were not the best lands. Much of the 200,000 acres was dry and rocky and without consistent sources of water. The lands that were most quickly allocated were small house lots, since farming often was not feasible where the agricultural lots were reserved.

And the blood quantum requirement had a fractionalizing aspect, serving to divide the native population along a line that had no respect for family, for generations within a family, or for cultural attachment.

*I*n 1917 Queen Lili'uokalani died. In 1922 Prince Kūhiō died. The last ties to our royal past were cut. We were adrift.

$\mathcal{B}$y 1922 there were only 24,000 pure Hawaiians left alive.

*F*oreign influence had fast become foreign domination. If we were to have a place in our own home it seemed that there were but two choices. We could retreat to the farthest reaches of the country and strive to live as much as possible in isolation, or we could assimilate, capitulate to the dominant culture, and strive to become a part of it.

The dominant society welcomed our assimilation. But in its heart of hearts the dominant society did not believe us competent or equal. As late as 1965 the influential Pacific Club did not allow Hawaiians to join its roster of members. And while bank tellers and loan officers might be of Hawaiian blood, bank presidents were white. The publishers of both daily newspapers were, and are to this day, white. The owners of radio stations were white. The CEOs of Hawai'i's major corporations were, and are to this day, white.

We might be managers and supervisors, but we were not decision makers. We could play a part, but we could not write the play.

*H*ollywood gave us images of ourselves, languid, lovely, romantic visions of Polynesian maidens blessed with narrow noses, thin lips, and pale skin, images many of us tried to recreate in beauty parlors and at home.

While we were buying western dresses from Liberty House, *kamaʻāina haole* women donned missionary-inspired muʻu's and put flowers in their hair to set themselves apart from our mainland and foreign visitors who, lei-bedecked in paper flowers, embarrassed us all with their excess and silly caricatures of Hawaiians in sarongs dancing naughty hulahulas to the beat of drums whose sound and rhythm had never before been heard in any part of Polynesia.

And then came the war.

*T*he war was cataclysm and catharsis; not a harbinger of change, but change itself. Now Hawai'i was irrevocably American, and we who were Hawaiian became American first and Hawaiian second.

On December 7, 1941, at a few minutes before eight in the morning, Pearl Harbor was attacked. Three-and-a-half hours later, at 11:30 A.M., martial law was declared in Hawai'i.

For the next three years Hawai'i was governed by the U.S. military. Constitutional rights were suspended for the duration. Courts were under military jurisdiction. The press was controlled—and censored—by the military. Garbage collection, labor regulation, traffic control, even the licensing of bowling alleys, were controlled by the military.

The Royal Hawaiian Hotel, the gracious queen of Waikīkī, exchanged her crown for a cap of khaki. In the suites where the wealthy once relaxed in rattan, now soldiers and sailors recuperated from the rigors of war. In the ballrooms where visiting aristocracy had waltzed, young men in uniform lindied with WACs and WAVEs.

$\mathcal{T}$he war brought soldiers and sailors by the tens of thousands. It also brought prosperity, and it brought photographers, writers, reporters, and filmmakers. Suddenly the entire world knew where Hawai'i was.

But we, the Hawaiian people, were not in the stories or photos or films. It was as though we were invisible, except as hula dancers and ukulele players to entertain the troops on leave.

$\mathcal{O}$n August 14, 1945, Japan surrendered and victory was declared.

The war was over, but the military stayed. The Naval Shipyard at Pearl Harbor; the U.S. Army Pacific Headquarters at Fort Shafter; Schofield Army Barracks; Wheeler Army Air Force Base; Bellows Air Force Field; Fort DeRussy; Fort Ruger; Kahuku Training Camp; and Lualualei Naval Ammunition Depot were on just the one 592.7 square mile island of Oʻahu. And they're still here.

*A*fter the war, change came faster and faster. Sugar and pineapple ruled, but tourism and the military were becoming the twin pillars of our economy. They were pillars made of sand.

Now we were American, but what did being American mean?

It meant soda pop, hot dogs, bebop, suburbs, two cars in every garage, Elvis Presley and Johnny Weissmuller, jobs from nine to five, white bread, the right to vote, church on Sunday, Doris Day, cocktail parties, personal ambition, the American Dream, and the guarantee of life, liberty, and the pursuit of happiness.

America prospered after the war. Americans in Hawai'i prospered, too. But Hawaiians on the whole were not prospering.

We wore American clothes, listened to American music, saluted the American flag. We were willing to sacrifice being Hawaiian if the sacrifice could make us prosperous Americans.

STATEHOOD!

House Sends Bill to Ike

WASHINGTON, D.C., March 12—Congress ended decades of procrastination today and sent to the White House a bill to give Hawaii the Statehood it has so long deserved.

The House overwhelmingly approved the bill this afternoon.

The vote was 323-89. The time was 3:04 p.m. E.S.T. (10:04 a.m. H.I.T.). It was the same bill that passed the Senate 76-15 last night.

More Statehood . . .
On Pages 1-A, 1-B

Whig Paper Urged Statehood in 1849

Many Changes Due In Status of Isles

Statehood Won OK's Four Times Before

Statehood Reasons Given Over Years

State Offices Lure Politicians

. . . On the inside

Question on Size Of State . . . Page 1-D

Two New Songs Mark Statehood . . . Page 5

Burns Eyes Senate Past . . . Page 1-D

Celebrations Sweep Honolulu . . . Page 2-A

Resolution Favors 'Aloha State' . . . Page 27

Governors Laud Isles . . . Page 5

Honolulu Star-Bulletin

HONOLULU, TERRITORY OF HAWAII, U. S. A., THURSDAY, MARCH 12, 1959

Honolulu Star-Bulletin, Vol. 48, No. 61   Phone 57-911

Special Radio, Phone Lines Flash News

Sirens, Bells Herald Statehood Arrival

DIRECTORY

Faubus's Telegram

★   ★   ★   First Class Citizens Now   ★   ★   ★

*O*n August 21, 1959, Hawai'i became the fiftieth state of the union. Now, surely, American prosperity would be ours. The American Dream would now be ours to pursue.

But it was not ours. The Dream eluded us, no matter how valiantly we pursued it.

It eluded us because it did not fit us. Our history was not America's history, our experience was not the American experience, and our culture remained apart from America's culture.

But we were quiet. We donned the ill-fitting garb of Americanism, but beneath the clothing we were still Hawaiian.

And in our effort to appear American, we sought to bury that which was Hawaiian. We reorganized our Hawaiianness to conform with tourism's and Hollywood's pictures of Hawaiians. We wore hula skirts of colored plastic, waved our hair and colored our lips to look like Dorothy Lamour, served tourists baked ham with pineapple, mixed drinks of Caribbean rum and gave them phony Polynesian names, smiled for the camera, and posed barebreasted for postcard art.

*H*awaiian discontent festered slowly beneath the bandages of Americanism we wore to deny and hide our wounds.

We were sickened by our wounds, and in time our sickness made us angry.

On the fourth of January, 1976, Hawaiian resistance broke through the surface. On that day, George Jarret Helm, Jr., Noa Emmett Aluli, Walter Ritte, Jr., and six other young Hawaiians illegally landed on the island of Kahoʻolawe to protest military use of Hawaiian land.

If the Dick and Jane books not going to make you proud of who you are, Kahoʻolawe is going to.

—George Jarrett Helm, Jr.

George Helm and the Protect Kahoʻolawe ʻOhana sought their vision for the future in the wisdom of the past. The struggle for Kahoʻolawe was as cultural as it was political. The leaders of the movement went to *kūpuna* and *kāhuna* for guidance that comes from the Hawaiian past and for advice to help restore what is Hawaiian for the present and the future.

For the next fourteen months, George Helm and other leaders of the Protect Kahoʻolawe ʻOhana dedicated their talents, hearts, and minds to securing freedom for Kahoʻolawe. They spoke in schools, at concerts, in the legislature of the State of Hawaiʻi.

On March 6, 1977, George Helm and Kimo Mitchell started once again for the island of Kahoʻolawe. They were never seen again.

With their disappearance a martyr was born and a movement galvanized.

*O*ne by one, and then by twos and threes and fours, people and groups rallied to the cause.

Save Mākua, Save Sand Island, Save Waimānalo, Save Anahola, Save Ka'ū, Save Wao Kele O Puna, Save Honokahua, Save Hālawa Valley, Save Sunset Beach, Save Miloli'i; Life of the Land, Pele Defense Fund, Ka 'Ohana o Ka Lae, Ka Lāhui Hawai'i, the Hawaiian Nation.

Hawaiian voices rose in protest, protest against wrongs done in the past, against abuse in the present, against the loss of Hawai'i in the future.

*I*n the 1970s and into the 1980s, "sovereignty" was a word spoken in whispers. Then the whispers grew and sovereignty was spoken aloud.

In 1992, the United States returned Kaho'olawe to the people of Hawai'i.

On January 17, 1993, ten thousand people converged on the grounds of 'Iolani Palace. The day marked the one-hundredth year since the overthrow of the Hawaiian Kingdom. And on the 17th of January, 1993, from the steps of the Palace where our last ruling queen had been made a prisoner in her own home, dignitaries read an official apology by the United States government for its illegal participation in the overthrow of our nation.

Now sovereignty is on the lips of Hawaiian and non-Hawaiian alike. Some utter it with a vengeance, some with hope, some with fear. Sovereignty is no longer just the dream of a few young Hawaiians.

$\mathcal{P}$hoto Credits

$\mathcal{B}$ibliography

Barrere, Dorothy B. *The Kumuhonua Legends*. Pacific Anthropological Records No. 3. Honolulu: Bernice P. Bishop Museum, 1969.

Bayley, Harold. *The Lost Language of Symbolism*. Escondido, Calif.: The Book Tree, 2000.

Beckwith, Martha Warren, trans. and ed. *The Kumulipo: A Hawaiian Creation Chant*. Honolulu: University of Hawai‘i Press, 1972.

Blaisdell, Richard Kekuni, M.D. "The Health Status of Kanaka Maoli (Indigenous Hawaiians)." *Asian American and Pacific Islander Journal of Health* 1, no. 2 (Autumn 1993).

Bushnell, O. A. *The Gifts of Civilization*. Honolulu: University of Hawai‘i Press, 1993.

Daws, Gavan. *Shoal of Time*. Honolulu: University of Hawai‘i Press, 1968.

De Santillana, Giorgio, and Hertha Von Dechend. *Hamlet's Mill*. Boston: David R. Godine, 1977.

Dye, Tom. "Population Trends in Hawai‘i Before 1778." *The Hawaiian Journal of History* 28 (1994).

Emerson, Nathaniel B. *Unwritten Literature of Hawaii*. Rutland, Vt.: Charles E. Tuttle Co., 1965.

Fornander, Abraham. *An Account of the Polynesian Race: Its Origin and Migrations, and the Ancient History of the Hawaiian People to the Times of Kamehameha I.* Vol. I. 1878. Reprint, Rutland, Vt.: Charles E. Tuttle Co., 1973.

———. *An Account of the Polynesian Race: Its Origin and Migrations, and the Ancient History of the Hawaiian People to the Times of Kamehameha I.* Vol. II. 1880. Reprinted as *Ancient History of the Hawaiian People to the Times of Kamehameha I,* Honolulu: Mutual Publishing, 1996.

Handy, E. S. Craighill, and Mary Kawena Pukui. *The Polynesian Family System in Ka'u, Hawai'i.* Rutland, Vt.: Charles E. Tuttle Co., 1977.

"The Health of Native Hawaiians." *Pacific Health Dialogue, Journal of Community Health and Clinical Medicine for the Pacific* 5, no. 2 (September 1998).

Johnson, Rubellite Kawena, and John Kaipo Mahelona. *Na Inoa Hoku.* Honolulu: Topgallant Publishing, 1975.

Kamakau, Samuel Manaiakalani. *Ka Po'e Kahiko.* Honolulu: Bishop Museum Press, 1964.

———. *Tales and Traditions of the People of Old.* Honolulu: Bishop Museum Press, 1991.

Kame'eleihiwa, Lilikala. *Nā Wāhine Kapu.* Honolulu: 'Ai Pōhaku Press, 1999.

Malo, David. *Hawaiian Antiquities.* Honolulu: Bishop Museum Press, 1951.

Marsella, A. J., J. M. Oliveira, C. M. Plummer, and K. M. Crabbe. "Native Hawaiian Culture, Mind, and Well-being." In *Resiliency in Ethnic Minority Families.* Vol. I, *Native and Immigrant American Families*, edited by H. I. McCubbin, E. A. Thompson, A. I. Thompson, and J. E. Fromer. Madison: University of Wisconsin Press, 1995.

Melville, Leinani. *Children of the Rainbow.* Wheaton, Ill.: The Theosophical Publishing House, 1969.

Meyer, Manulani Aluli. "Native Hawaiian Epistemology." Ph.D. diss., Harvard University, 1998.

Morales, Rodney. *Ho'iho'i Hou.* Honolulu: Bamboo Ridge Press, 1984.

Pukui, Mary Kawena, and Samuel H. Elbert. *Hawaiian Dictionary,* rev. and enl. ed. Honolulu: University of Hawai'i Press, 1986.

Sahlins, Marshall. *How Natives Think.* Chicago: University of Chicago Press, 1995.

Valeri, Valerio. *Kingship and Sacrifice.* Chicago: University of Chicago Press, 1985.